Glow In The Dark

Grace Bonallie

BookLeaf Publishing

Presentation by *BookLeaf Publishing*

Web: www.bookleafpub.com

E-mail: info@bookleafpub.com

ISBN: 9789357446235

First edition 2022

DEDICATION

A great deal of people have contributed to the words on these pages, some will never know of their influence. Those I wish to thank are BookLeaf Publishing for giving me this opportunity in the first place. Richie, for being my saviour. Darcie and Robyn, for being the reason I am here. My amazing friends, Sally, Emma, Paula and Claire, for being my biggest supporters and getting me through some of the hardest times of my life. Kimberley, Lindsey and Paul of Bishop Auckland College for facilitating a huge journey of growth. My clients who inspire me every day. And my family, who have all contributed towards the various emotions behind the words. To you, the reader, I thank you for being here with me.

ACKNOWLEDGE MENT

For Richie, Darcie and Robyn, forever my inspirations.

PREFACE

It is by chance that this collection of poems is sitting in your lap right now. It had been on my bucket list for some time to become a published author, to write a book before it's my time, but poetry had never been my thing. You may now be wondering why I wrote a book of poems. And well the answer is, I saw an opportunity and I took it. I entered a challenge, to write 21 poems in 21 days, and that's exactly what this book is. The challenge really came with what to write 21 poems about. And my inspiration stemmed from life experiences of myself and those I have encountered. I am training to become a therapist, and have seen the true beauty of what therapy can achieve. Not everyone will agree and that is fine, but for me, the journey has been life-saving, and I wanted to share that growth and strength with my readers. My hope for this book is that it can inspire someone to do what they have been putting off, it can help someone get through a dark moment or two, or simply, it can give someone a break, from parenting, working, cleaning, overthinking! Whatever this book does for you, even if it does nothing, I just want you to enjoy it. So take a moment, have a flick through, and let your mind escape for a few.

Bury The Hatchet

Today I made a new friend,
I've known her for a while,
She has always been around,
But in the past, I've been hostile.

My friend has taught me things,
Raised questions about myself,
That I've avoided for so long,
To protect my mental health.

But shielding from those teachings,
Has taught me no lesson,
It's time I face the facts,
And leave behind the suppression.

I'll take the hand of my new friend,
As I embark on a fresh journey,
She can guide me through greater depths,
Without letting fear deter me.

My new friend is called Sadness,
And we are in this together,
I can't get through life without her,
She is the reason for my pleasure.

She makes me feel alive,
Without her, who would I be?
I'd be caged without contentment,
Sadness has set me free.

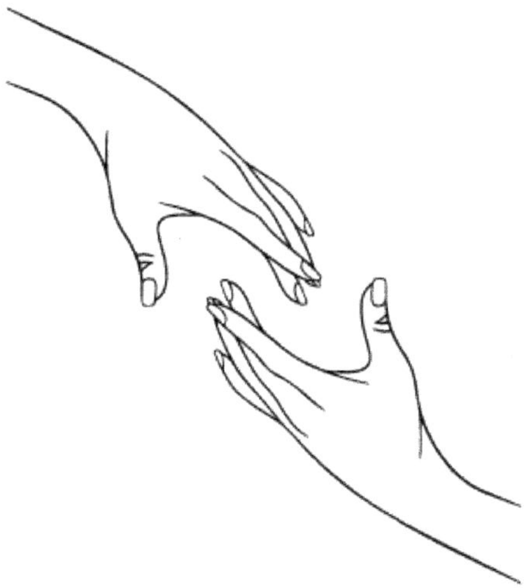

Blues

And here you are, in my arms,
A weight so light I can barely muster the strength to hold it,
But hold it I must,
For I have no choice, you are here, in my arms.

And here you are, lying next to me,
A face so deep sleeping easily,
But easy this is not,
For I feel pain while you are here, lying next to me.

And here you are, screaming for me,
A sound so loud I can no longer hear it,
But hear it should,
For I am accountable, you are here, screaming for me.

And here you are, smiling with glee,
A smile so infectious I don't catch it,
But catch it I wish to,
For I feel numb, you are here, smiling with glee.

And here I am, where am I?

And here I am, what am I doing?
And here I am, why do I feel this way?
And here I am, who have I become?

And here you are, perfect in every way,
A gem so precious I forgot to treasure you,
But treasure you I do,
For I adore you, you are here, perfect in every way.

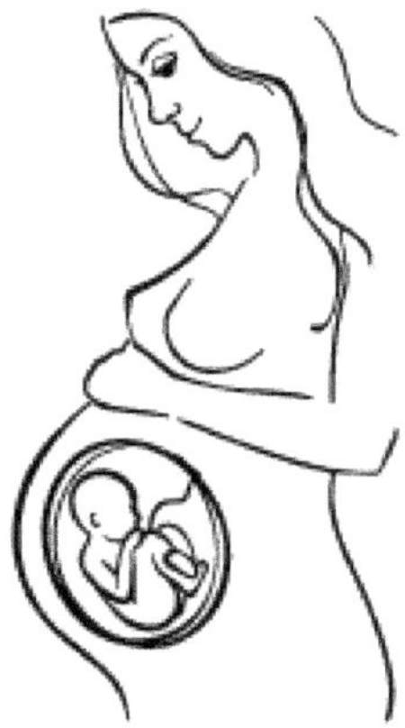

Not a Victim

For what?
For control, for power, for a thrill?
For what?
For you to live your fantasy while I lay there still?
You know what?
The excuse never mattered
You know what?
I'm not the slightest bit flattered
And why?
Because I am not your possession
And why?
Because I am worthy despite your oppression

I stopped asking questions,
Because no reason will ever suffice,
Always my fault, I gave the impressions,
My sanity I will no longer sacrifice,
You have no power, no control, no thrill,
Your fantasy cut short,
Because I won't be silenced nor lay still,
My truth will see you in court,
I am a survivor, you see,

And I have been empowered,
You cannot break nor defeat me,
For you are just a coward.

Stages

Don't say it.
Everything is fine, I just know it.
No... no...... NO.
It just can't be, can it?
All the things we had planned, I don't believe it.
Losing you? No, I won't have it.

After I told you to take care of yourself!
Now, what do I do?
Great things you had intended for yourself!
Everything that we have been through!
Rage is burning within myself!

Because it should have been me, my past is checkered.
All I need is a little more time, please!
Rid me of this pain and I promise I will do better.
God, if you are there, please!
Ache in my heart is unbearable
I need to be free from this, please!
Never felt anything so insufferable.
I need to breathe again, please!
Now I promise I do believe,
God, if you can hear me, please.

Deathly silence
Echoing through my mind
Please just leave me be
Really, I don’t need guidance
Emptiness has my soul confined
Sleep is calling for me
So, leave behind your condolence
I do not intend to be unkind
Obligatory sympathy won’t set me free
Now just leave me in silence.

And now, time has passed,
Cliché to say that time can heal,
Couldn’t imagine myself in this place,
Eventually, I am here.
Precious memories of when we talked last,
Treasured where it stays real,
And I know I’ll never again see your face,
Nevertheless, it remains clear.
Constant thoughts of you pass each day,
Eternally here you will stay.

Love From Your Beautiful Mind

Deep breaths, come on we can do this,
Together in arms, we can reminisce,
About a time that we were calm and in control,
Let us reconnect with your beautiful soul.

I am strong, say it with me,
While envisioning the tranquil sea,
Breathe in the crisp, fresh air,
Come on, together we will get there.

Go to your safe place, where is that for you?
Is it a mountain top with a spectacular view?
Perhaps it's a field full of cheerful sunflowers,
Wherever it be, we can go, we have the power!

That was then, and this is now,
We can heal if you'll allow,
This too shall pass, like all that has before,
We do not have to suffer anymore.

Just like the seasons and the changes they bring,
The bitterness of winter, the hope of the spring,

The freedom of summer, the welcoming fall,
Each passing phase, we push through them all,

I am here with you each step of the way,
You are never alone, even on the loneliest day,
We will soldier on, together in comradery,
This war, we fight with courage and bravery.

Who am I?

Who am I?
A composition of breath, blood and bones.
Who am I?
A mind, a body, a soul.
Who am I?
A heart that beats and loves and breaks.
Who am I?
A living being capable of making mistakes.
Who am I?
Beyond a tale of birth and background.
Who am I?
Beyond what I believe I am bound.
Who am I?
Beyond a debate of nature or nurture.
Who am I?
Beyond tales of wild adventure.
Who am I?
When I am entirely alone.
Who am I?
When I am not fulfilling a role.
Who am I?
When there is no pressure or judgement.
Who am I?
When I do not fear embarrassment.
Who am I?

Will I ever really know?
Who am I?
Will there be an end to my show?
Who am I?
Will I succeed in self-actualisation?
Who am I?
Will I view myself with admiration?
Who am I?
I am a human with strengths I wouldn't believe.
Who am I?
I am a human with so much to achieve.
Who am I?
I am a human who is on a journey with a
purpose.
Who am I?
I am a human who will never be worthless.

She Hides It Well

Morning love, are you hungry?
I made some porridge with lots of honey!
Just the way you like it, won't you have some?
"I'll grab something later, sorry Mum."

Hey friend, I brought some cakes as a treat,
You could use one, you are so petite!
There are chocolate ones, here you go!
"Oh I had a big breakfast, thanks though!"

Hello busy bee, have you got time for a bite?
You've not had lunch all week so I thought you might,
We could go to that café you like if you want?
"Can we raincheck, sorry it's just I am swamped!"

Welcome home darling, smells good don't you agree!
I made your favourite dish, you deserve a treat!
You've barely eaten lately, you have so much to juggle,
"Maybe just a little bowl, since you went to so much trouble"

Sweetheart, are you okay? You've been in there a while!
If you are feeling unwell, I can make some tea with chamomile,
Was it the food, you can be honest!
"Don't worry, I'm fine, I promise."

Talking is Healing

I have my first therapy session today,
And I am nervous to say the least,
I have no idea what to expect,
But it is time to tame this beast,
That bellows in the darkest corner,
Deep inside my mind,
I can't go on like this,
To myself I must be kind.

I had my first therapy session today!
And wow…what a relief,
I got so much off my chest,
That I already feel less grief,
Don't get me wrong, I know,
That this is the first tiny step,
But it is in the right direction,
Because I finally asked for help.

I had my third therapy session today,
And we really poked the bear,
We dug right to the root cause,
Of why he lives in there,
He is there because I allowed him to be,
But I am raising the rent,

He will not have it easy anymore,
At the cost of my content.

I have my last therapy session today,
And I am overwhelmed with emotion,
I feel like it has been a long process,
Of which I have gushed with devotion,
I have laid myself bare in that room,
And have been met with empathy,
It is time I put to use the tools,
That have been given as my remedy.

I had my last therapy session,
It must have been about a year ago,
And I am utterly proud to say,
My how much I have grown,
The life I am now able to lead,
Feels like a total rebirth,
Because now I can finally see,
All that I am truly worth.

Hear Me

Do you listen to me?
You may think that you do,
But you don’t hear me,
If you force your view.
Do you listen to me?
Give it a moment’s thought,
Because you don’t hear me,
If I don't have your support.
Do you listen to me?
Do you really understand?
Because you don’t hear me,
If you have my answer planned.
Do you listen to me?
To the emotion behind my words,
Because you don’t hear me,
If you push your concerns.
Do you listen to me?
Not to respond but to hear,
Because you don’t hear me,
If your opinions interfere.
Do you listen to me?
I know it’s hard to stay reserved,
But to really hear me,
Is what I deserve.

A Haiku To Remind You

Emotional care
Is just as important as
Physical welfare.

It Doesn't Just Happen To Soldiers

They say that soldiers who fought in the war,
Get flashbacks that change who they were before,
But I have never been in battle,
So why does my mind feel shackled,
Chained to the memory of a time I'd rather ignore,
But I have to stay there and still I endure,
The pain, the hurt, the ringing in my ears,
The precise exact moment I felt true fear,
I can't escape not even in my sleep,
Because in my nightmares it continues to creep,
My days feel like an incessant migraine,
It feels as if I've nothing left to gain,
I am stuck in the past so how can I move on,
The war in my mind has already been won.

Circle of Anxiety

I can't eat, I can't sleep, I can't think, I can't
rest,
Rest just fills me with so much guilt,
Guilt because I just don't deserve it,
It feels like I never do enough,
Enough to please everyone all of the time,
Time just goes by so fast yet so slow,
Slow enough to let me know that I am failing,
Failing at this storm that you call life,
Life is not the same experience for everyone,
Everyone seems to misjudge who I am,
Am I ever going to rid this feeling?
Feeling like I am pointless,
Pointless without a purpose.

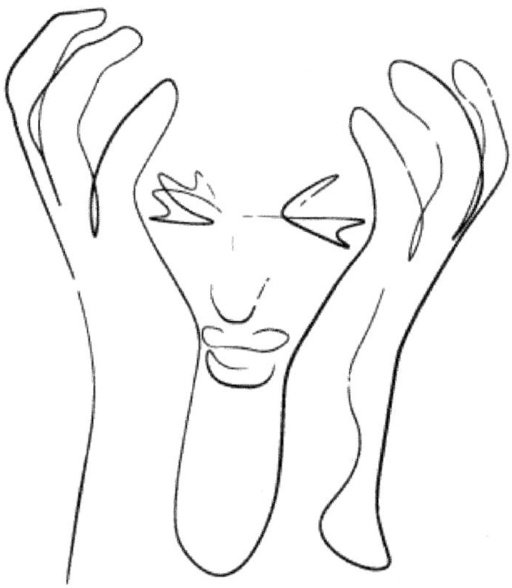

Worthy

You are enough!
You always will be!
No matter what anyone tells you.
You are enough!
You always will be!
No matter what you have been through.
You are enough!
You always will be!
No matter the opinions of others.
You are enough!
You always will be!
No matter how much you've suffered.
You are enough!
You always will be!
My darling I wish you could see.
That you are enough!
And you always will be!
Let yourself be free.

Gone But Not Forgotten

Sometimes I miss her,
And I feel shame when this thought occurs,
Childlike innocence and wholesome naivety,
That I wished away and now I envy,
And these thoughts when they come,
I don't know where they are from,
Because I am happy, I swear,
Sometimes it just feels unfair,
That I have so much on my shoulders now,
And I am riddled with constant self-doubt,
She didn't have any responsibility,
She was wild and young and utterly free,
But I guess life now is more purposeful,
I am no longer a sheep, I am a wolf!
Sometimes I miss her, but she has grown,
Into a strong woman, who stands on her own

Sudden Attack

Faster and faster
My breath and my heart
I can't catch myself
Before the start
Faster and faster
My mind races with panic
I am completely out of control
The world suddenly seems manic
Faster and faster
My whole body is shaking
A moment never-ending
Of which there is no escaping
Faster and faster
The sweat coats my palms
While some useless voice echoes
"Just try and be calm!"

Be Kind to Your Mind

Would you tell someone,
Diagnosed with cancer,
To just get over it,
Expecting that to be the answer?
Would you tell someone,
With a broken bone,
To just snap out of it,
And that they shouldn't moan?
The it that you are afraid to define,
Is called mental illness,
And it attacks the mind.
It is just as debilitating,
As your flu or your stomach-ache,
Only it's constant and doesn't ease,
With a few lazy relaxing days.
A healthy body is nothing,
Without a healthy soul,
Care for your mind as it is also a temple,
Allow it space to thrive and grow.

One to Ponder

Let me ask you a question…
Can you think of your closest friend?

Good, now…

Your friend has come to you with an issue,
An issue they don't expect you to mend,
Just for you to listen to,
And that is exactly what you do,
You listen to the issue,
And you offer your support,
And you are kind and soft,
You care so much for your friend,
And you would never condescend,
You know your friend does not deserve,
To feel so low and internally disturbed.

So let me ask you another question…

What if your friend was your mind?
Would you be so kind?

If not…
Then why?

Treat yourself the same way you would treat
your friend,
Because only on yourself you can truly depend,
Forever and always,
Entwined together as one,
Be gentle with yourself because,
You are as vital as the sun.

Look After Yourself

Have you ever heard of self-care?
It seems to be somewhat rare
That we take a step back
To really relax
And offer ourselves a chance to repair.

Self-care is understanding when you need a
break
Understanding that it is okay to escape
At least for a while
Allowing a smile
And it may even involve cake!

Self-care is knowing your boundaries and limits
What is worth your precious time and what isn't
You can't please everyone
It simply can't be done
Give yourself space and take a minute.

Self-care is letting go of what is toxic
Of people in your life that are truly narcotic
Of people that serve you no purpose
And make you feel worthless
Unburdening toxicity is perfectly logic.

Now you have heard what self-care consists of

I’m sure you can understand the importance of the above
Do whatever works for you
If it helps you feel new
As long as you shower yourself with deserving love.

A Haiku To Let You Know

It’s okay to cry
To feel emotion is to
Be truly alive.

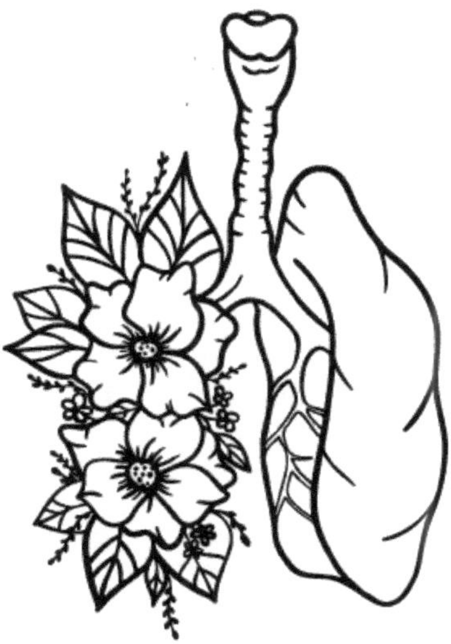

You Can't Fight Pain With Pain

The world is too loud,
So, I go to my room,
Where I am alone,
In deathly silence.
But the deathly silence,
It begins to speak to me,
It tells me the truth,
About myself.
I am not good enough;
I don't look like her;
I am not smart nor clever;
I possess no talents.
And I believe it,
The pain penetrates me,
And it builds up,
And I need to release,
But I am alone,
In deathly silence.
And I cry and I cry,
But it is not enough,
Just like me,
So, I use pain to release
But the agony persists.

ABCs Of Recovery

Attention please!
Because I have an important message to convey,
Coming out of the other side stronger than
before,
Deserves some recognition for sure,
Even though you may feel like it's no
achievement,
Future you is sending out a letter of thanks,
Go out and scream and shout,
How much you have grown without a doubt,
In a years' time you'll look back in awe,
Joyous memories of how far you have come,
Kites can't even fly as high as you now,
Look at the incredible journey you have been on,
Mountains were moved,
Nothing is in your way,
Only a path of your destiny lies ahead,
Paved only by what you desire,
Queries you have are solved with ease,
Risks are taken but only at your will,
So, take your own hand and guide the way,
Towards the future that you have the power to
create,
Utter control is waiting for you,

Vow to take care of yourself each step of the way,
Wonder what life can be like without pain,
Xenagogue to yourself you are,
You my dear have the strength and direction to,
Zestfully live on through whatever is next for you.

www.ingramcontent.com/pod-product-compliance
Lightning Source LLC
Chambersburg PA
CBHW051739130826
49812CB00033B/926
* 9 7 8 9 3 5 7 4 4 6 2 3 5 *